Acknowledgements

We would like to initiate this section by expressing our sincere gratitude to the Almighty, the Source of all guidance, as well as to our beloved Imam Al-Mahdi(as), whose prayers enabled us to complete this small effort.

Like any other project, this was a result of the collaborative effort of many individuals. Without their help and support this book wouldn't have come into existence. The following individuals deserve to be highlighted here.

Sayyid Hashim Al Bahrani - for *Al Burhan fi tafsīr*.
Salam al Tamimi - the author of *The Luminous Flashes* which became the source and inspiration of this book. *The Luminous Flashes* is a translation of volume 4 of *Al Burhan fi tafsīr*
Masooma Ali - for providing us with her invaluable advice, initial editing and cheering throughout the process.
Amy Claire Nelson - the editor, for providing her valuable time to review and improve the text on short notice.
Kashaf Fatima - the illustrator, for her wonderful work on the front cover.
Our parents & family - who supported us through many late nights, especially my father **Syed Misbah ur Raza** who envisioned and encouraged us to publish this piece.

May Allah(swt) forgive our shortcomings, accept the work for all who contributed towards this project and keep them protected.

Comments and Feedback
reflect.fourteen@gmail.com
Instagram: reflect_14

Photos
Imam Ali.net, Unsplash.com, Syed Jeem, Pixabay.com, Freeislamiccalligraphy.com, Ali Bahraini

References
https://www.imamali.net/?id=2561
https://imam-us.org/islamic-awareness/islam-101/beliefs/ahl-al-bayt/imam-ali-ibn-abi-talib
https://english.khamenei.ir/news/7550/The-father-of-the-orphans
http://www.alseraj.net/maktaba/kotob/english/FourteenInfallibles/ABiographical/ahlulbayt14/imam-ali.html#a17

Copyright
ALL RIGHTS RESERVED. ANY PART OF THIS PUBLICATION MAY BE USED WITHOUT CONSENT.

The Father of Orphans

والد الآيتام

In the name of God,
the Most Gracious, the Most Merciful

وَيُطْعِمُونَ الطَّعَامَ عَلَىٰ حُبِّهِ مِسْكِينًا وَيَتِيمًا وَأَسِيرًا

For the love of Him, they feed the needy, the orphan, and the prisoner.

QUR'AN 76:8

To all the orphans around the world who are waiting for a guardian like Imam Ali (as).

Table of Contents

Prologue 8
Virtues of Imam Ali (as) 10

LEADERSHIP

The One Who Guides with Truth and Establishes Justice 13
The Guardian of Believers 14
A Guide for All 17
The One Who is Purified by Allah 18
A Clear Register 20
Declaration of Imam Ali's Succession 21
Instruction about the Announcement 23
Announcement of Imam Ali's Succession 24

GENEROSITY

Imam Ali's Charity 29
Voluntary Donor 30
Maintainer of Zakat 31
The One Whose Charity is Accepted 32
Giver of Charity 33

DEVOTION

Remembering Allah in Times of Affliction 37
Receiver of Allah's Blessings 38
Attaining Allah's Pleasure on the Night of Hijrah 39
The Soul of Rasulullah (s) 40
Being Amongst The Virtuous 42
Trusting in the Power of Allah 44
The One Who is Loved by Allah 45

❋ KINDNESS

Giving Charity in Difficult Times 49

The Helper of Poor and Orphans 50

The One Who is Remembered as Kindness 51

❋ SPIRITUALITY

Acceptance of Islam 55

The Rope of Allah 56

Allah's Grace 57

Knower of Secrets 57

The Straight Path 58

A Caller on the Day of Judgement 59

Allah's Light 60

The Divider of Heaven and Hell 63

Purifier For Hearts 64

Allah's Help 65

Epilogue 67

Prologue

"Fear God when the question of helpless orphans arises. You should not let them be full some times and hungry at other times. So long as you are there to guard and protect them, they should not be ruined or lost."

—ALI IBN ABI TALIB (AS)

Whenever we utter the name of Ali ibn Abi Talib(as), a vision of a valorous warrior appears in our minds. However, there are many aspects of his personality that go unrecognized compared to the attention he gets for his skills on the battlefield. All of the other characteristics he exhibited, particularly his devotion and unconditional love for the orphans of his time, are just as important as his warrior image. It is due to Imam Ali's supreme insight that he gave himself the title "The Father of Orphans." When he would instruct orphans, "If someone asks you 'who is your father?' tell them it's Ali ibn Abi Talib," he was offering them protection from the oppressors of society.

Abu Tufayl narrates that Imam Ali(as) used to project such love towards the orphans that he would say, "I am the father of the orphans. I must show compassion to them so that I will have treated them as a father." Abu Tufayl continues, "Imam Ali(as) had put honey in the mouths of the orphans with his own hands so many times that one of the companions of that time said, 'I had wished I was an orphan too so that I would have received the same attention and kindness from the Commander of the Faithful(as).'"

During his governance, Imam Ali(as) gave special instructions to Malik al-Ashtar (as related in *Tuhaf al-'Uqul*), "Take upon yourself the upkeep of the orphans and aged from among those who have no means at their disposal, and do not allow them to exert themselves in begging. Arrange pensions for them. They are the servants of Allah."

To some, the title "The Father of Orphans" might paint a picture of someone who was simply a humanitarian in society or a person who didn't engage in other socio-political matters. This, however, could not be further from the truth. Imam Ali(as) was favored with many virtues which he manifested over the course of his life. Through his spirituality, devotion and leadership, Imam Ali(as) fulfilled his role as helper and protector to not only Rasulullah(s) but also to the greater society. While he possessed numerous traits, Imam Ali(as) wished to be called "The Father of Orphans." Perhaps by choosing this title, Imam Ali(as) was instructing us to reflect on his soft nature and special connection towards those who were easy targets for abuse in society. Perhaps through this title he wanted us not only to keep an eye on the most deserving of the community, but to lend them a hand in times of need as well.

When we visualize the traits of a father, we realize the complexity of this personality. A father is an embodiment of love, kindness, integrity and devotion. He is the child's first guardian and role model who leaves a lasting impression of his leadership. This book is an attempt to highlight some of the traits of Imam Ali(as) that Allah has recognized in the Holy Qur'an; traits which helped the Imam(as) establish this title. We pray that, with the blessings of Allah, this will serve as a beneficial means for knowing and understanding the personality of "The Father of Orphans."

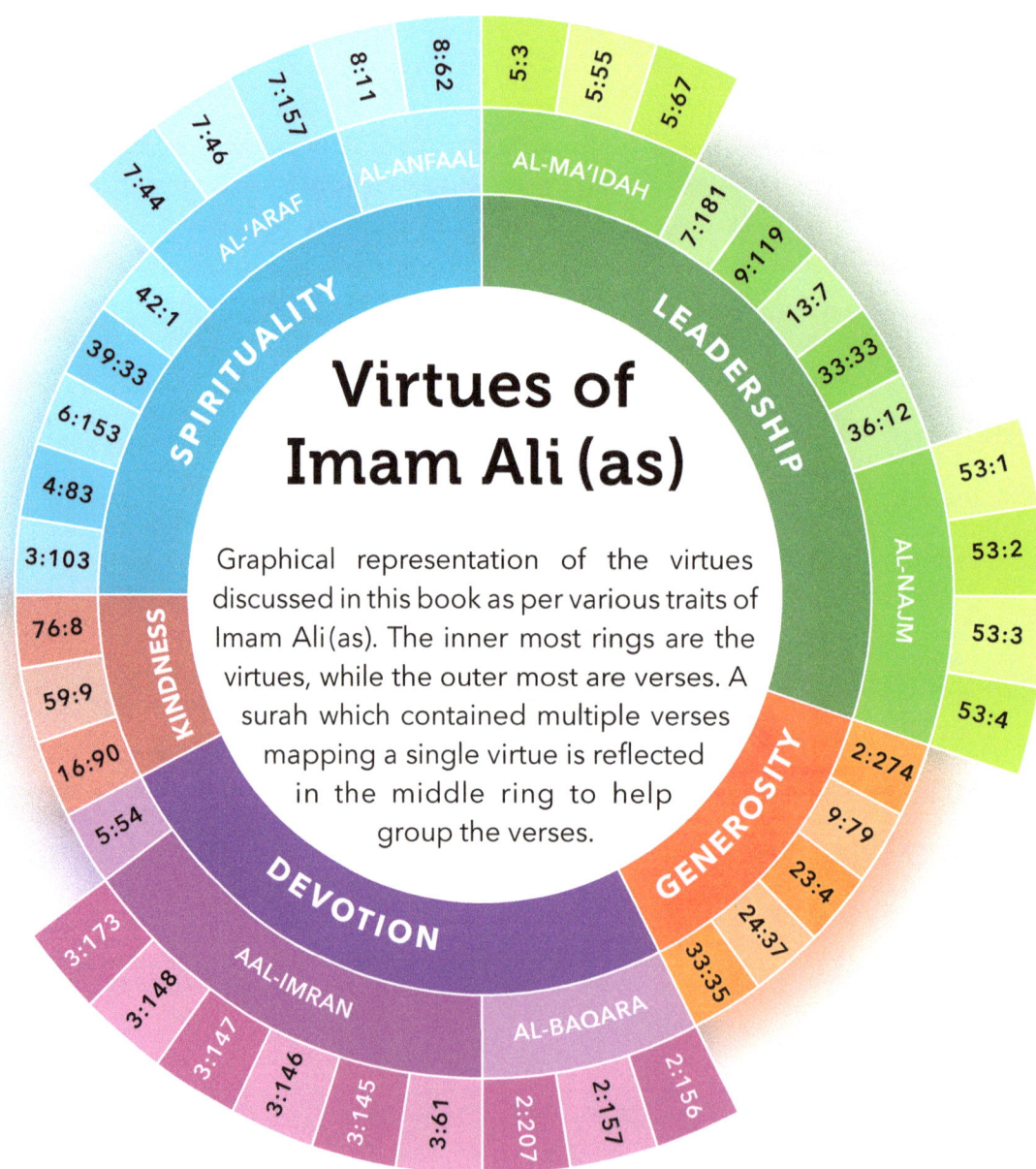

10 | *The Father of Orphans*

Leadership

The foundation of a rule
is to make use of leniency.

—ALI IBN ABI TALIB (AS)

LEADERSHIP

Leadership begins with trust and mastery. A divine leader is the one whose actions are in line with what he preaches. It is one of the special attributes which is given to only a few in history. Throughout the history of mankind, Allah chose some **Prophets** and **12 Imams** to lead their communities so that they would be guided towards the blessed path.

As the father of orphans, Imam Ali(as) exhibited God-given leadership skills through a system which solved the pertinent issues of the orphans at the time. In the short span of his governance, he reestablished the special office for the collection of alms and charities which were then spent on orphans, widows and other deserving members of the community. He handpicked the officers to ensure transparency for the allocations of funds. Along with providing monetary support, Imam Ali(as) would continually visit, engage, and counsel the orphans. He would often say to his companions, "They have lost their loving father, so cheer them up and treat them as a father."

The Holy Qur'an points towards the characteristics of true leadership in order to ease our doubts about its establishment. Divine Leadership is protected by Allah in order to keep His guidance purified for His creation. The verses in this section not only indicate the essential qualities of the leader, but explain how Imam Ali(as) was the rightly guided leader for the ummah after Rasulullah(s).

The One Who Guides with Truth and Establishes Justice

وَمِمَّنْ خَلَقْنَا أُمَّةٌ يَهْدُونَ بِالْحَقِّ وَبِهِ يَعْدِلُونَ

Among those We have created, is a community which guides by the truth and thereby establishes justice.

SURAH AL-A'RAF, VERSE: 181

Zadhan reported from Imam Ali(as) that he had said, "This community will be divided into 73 sects, out of which 72 will be in the Fire and one will be in the Garden. This verse indicates that group which is me and my followers."

In *Kashf al-Ghummah*, Ali ibn Isa reported from Imam Ali(as) that Rasulullah(s) was sitting in a gathering with him when he said, "O Ali! You bear a likeness to Jesus; some people loved him so much that they perished accordingly, and some hated him so much that they perished." Upon hearing that, some hypocrites said, "Can you not choose a likeness for him other than Jesus?"

Hence this verse was revealed as an answer to them.

Sources: *The Luminous Flashes* (212th Name), *Al-Burhan*, vol.2, p.53

The Guardian of Believers

إِنَّمَا وَلِيُّكُمُ اللَّهُ وَرَسُولُهُ وَالَّذِينَ آمَنُوا الَّذِينَ يُقِيمُونَ الصَّلَاةَ وَيُؤْتُونَ الزَّكَاةَ وَهُمْ رَاكِعُونَ

Your guardian is only Allah, His Apostle and the faithful who maintain the prayers and give the zakat while bowing down.

SURAH AL-MA'IDAH, VERSE: 55

This verse is also known as the **"Al-Wilayah Verse"** and has been referred to as a proof for the Wilayah/Leadership of Imam Ali (as).

The Father of Orphans

It is reported from Ali Ibn Hatam that once Rasulullah(s) was approached by a group of Jews who had professed Islam. They asked, "O Prophet of God! Moses(as) appointed Yushi Ibn Nun as his executor. Who do you appoint as your executor and who will be our guardian?" Thereupon this verse was revealed to Rasulullah(s), so he asked them to stand up and brought them to the entrance of the mosque. All of a sudden, a beggar came forth. Rasulullah(s) stopped him and had the following conversation:

Rasulullah(s): *"O beggar! Hasn't anyone given you anything?"*

Beggar: *"Yes indeed! This ring!"*

Rasulullah(s): *"Who has given it to you?"*

The beggar replied while pointing towards Imam Ali(as): *"That man who is praying has given it to me.."*

Rasulullah(s): *"In which state has he given it to you?"*

Beggar: *"He was bowing down."*

Rasulullah(s) exclaimed, *"God is the greatest,"* and so did the people of the mosque.

Rasulullah(s) said: *"Ali is your guardian after me."*

Sources: *The Luminous Flashes* (186th Name), *Al-Burhan*, vol.1, p.485

THE RING
Some facts about the ring which was given by Imam Ali(as)

GIVEN ON
24th of Dul al-Hijjah.

PREVIOUSLY BELONGED TO
Miran ibn Tawq who was slain by Imam Ali(as). It was submitted to Rasulullah(s) as the spoils of war.

WEIGHT
Four miskals (19.2 grams)

PRICE
Equivalent to the land tax of Syria (300 loads of silver and 4 loads of gold)

GIFTED TO IMAM ALI(AS) BY
Rasulullah(s)

In *Sirr al-Alamin*, Al Ghazali mentioned that the ring which Imam Ali(as) gave as charity belonged to Prophet Sulaiman(as).

The Truthful One

يَا أَيُّهَا الَّذِينَ آمَنُوا اتَّقُوا اللَّهَ وَكُونُوا مَعَ الصَّادِقِينَ

O you who have faith! Be wary of Allah, and be with the Truthful.

SURAH AT-TAWBAH, VERSE: 119

One of the essential characteristics of a leader is truthfulness. A true leader always fulfills his commitments to his community. Similarly, when a father promises something to his kids, it becomes incumbent upon him to follow through. As the father of orphans, Imam Ali(as) made sure never to break his promises to them. Therefore, he always remained true to his word in his dealings with everyone and especially with the impoverished. It is because of this commendable conduct that Allah remembers him as the truthful one.

In relation to this verse, Sulaym ibn Qays reported that the Commander of the Faithful(as) said, "When this verse was revealed, Salman inquired about the identification of the truthful one from Rasulullah(s). 'Is it general or specific?' he asked. Rasulullah(s) replied, 'As for the common people, they are ordered to be with the truthful believers. However, the truthful are specifically my brother Ali and my executors until the Day of Resurrection.'"

A Guide for All

وَيَقُولُ ٱلَّذِينَ كَفَرُوا لَوْلَا أُنزِلَ عَلَيْهِ ءَايَةٌ مِّن رَّبِّهِ ۗ إِنَّمَا أَنتَ مُنذِرٌ ۖ وَلِكُلِّ قَوْمٍ هَادٍ

The faithless say, "Why has not some sign been sent down to him from his Lord?" You are only a warner, and there is a guide for all people.

SURAH AR-RA'D, VERSE: 7

Abu Hamza al-Thumali narrated from Imam Muhammad Baqir(as) that when this verse was revealed to Rasulullah(s), he pointed towards himself and said "I am the warner." Then he held Imam Ali's(as) hand and said, "O Ali! You are the root of religion, the lighthouse of faith, the goal to guidance and the leader of the believers. I testify thereto in your favor."

Abd ibn Abdullah once reported that Imam Ali(as) said, "There is not a single verse revealed in the Qur'an without me knowing where it was revealed, concerning whom it was revealed and wherein it was revealed." He was asked, "What was then revealed concerning you?" He replied, "If it weren't for the fact that you asked me, I would never tell you." Then he recited this verse and said, "Rasulullah(s) is the warner and I am the guide to what he has brought."

The One Who is Purified by Allah

إِنَّمَا يُرِيدُ اللَّهُ لِيُذْهِبَ عَنكُمُ الرِّجْسَ أَهْلَ الْبَيْتِ وَيُطَهِّرَكُمْ تَطْهِيرًا

Indeed Allah desires to repel all impurity from you, O People of the Household, and purify you with a thorough purification.

SURAH AL-AHZAAB, VERSE: 33

This verse refers to the occasion when Rasulullah(s) visited the house of Syeda Fatimah(sa) and thereupon felt some weakness. Syeda Fatimah(sa) covered him with a cloak upon his request. Rasulullah(s) later gathered all the family members under his cloak and said, "O Allah! These are the members of my family. Keep impurities away from them and make them pure." Hence this verse was revealed as a testimony of their pure souls.

Ibn Babawayh reports from various narrations that Imam Ali(as) was present in the house of Umm Salma when this verse was revealed. Rasulullah(s) addressed him and said, "O Ali this verse refers to you and my two grandsons and the Imams from among your descendants." When Imam Ali(as) inquired further, Rasulullah(s) named all the Imams(as) from his progeny and said, "Their names are written upon the trunk of the Throne. When I asked God (exalted be He) about that, He replied, saying, 'These are the Imams after you; they are pure and infallible, while their enemies are cursed.'"

> Infallibility is an essential characteristic amongst the chosen leaders of mankind. Divine guidance is assured only through purity and the protection of Allah. Hence, the pure, infallible leader becomes a true channel of guidance for us.

Sources: *The Luminous Flashes* (612th- 614th Name), Al-islam.org

VERSE OF PURIFICATION

MEANING OF AL-RIJS الرِّجْس
The word Al-Rijs covers any impurity from the following categories and more:
- Spiritual
- Material
- Moral
- Ethical

HADITH AL-KISA

NARRATED BY
Jabir ibn Ansari (ra)

ATTENDEES*
1. Prophet Muhammad (s)
2. Ali ibn Abi Talib (as)
3. Syeda Fatimah (sa)
4. Al-Hasan (as)
5. Al-Hussain (as)
6. Ume Salma (ra)
7. Gabriel (as)
8. Mikaeel (as)

*As referred in tafsīr of Suyuti

Ibn Abbas reports that after this event, Rasulullah (s) would go to Imam Ali's (as) house at the time of prayers, address his family as his *Ahlul Bayt (People of the household)* and recite the covenant of Allah in this verse. He did this 5 times a day for nine months straight!

A Clear Register

إِنَّا نَحْنُ نُحْيِي الْمَوْتَىٰ وَنَكْتُبُ مَا قَدَّمُوا وَآثَارَهُمْ ۚ وَكُلَّ شَيْءٍ أَحْصَيْنَاهُ فِي إِمَامٍ مُبِينٍ

Indeed it is We who revive the dead and write what they have sent ahead and their effects [which they left behind], and We have figured everything in a clear register.

SURAH YASEEN, VERSE: 12

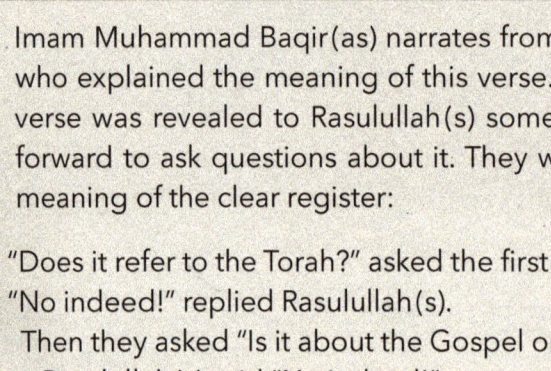

Imam Muhammad Baqir(as) narrates from Imam Hussain(as) who explained the meaning of this verse. He said, when this verse was revealed to Rasulullah(s) some companions went forward to ask questions about it. They wanted to know the meaning of the clear register:

"Does it refer to the Torah?" asked the first companion. "No indeed!" replied Rasulullah(s).
Then they asked "Is it about the Gospel or the Qur'an?" Rasulullah(s) said "No indeed!"

Thereupon Imam Ali(as) came forward to Rasulullah(s) and he said to his companions, "Look at that one! He is the Register wherein God (blessed and exalted be He) has numbered and kept knowledge of all things."

The Father of Orphans

Sources: *The Luminous Flashes* (652nd Name)

Declaration of Imam Ali's Succession

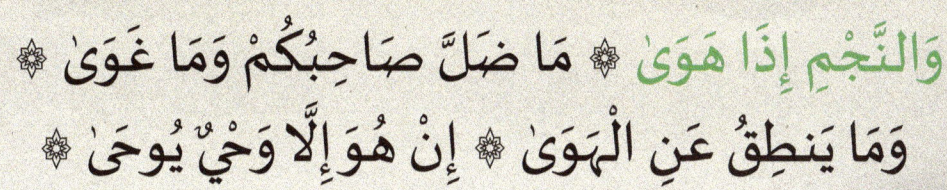

By the star when it sets. Your companion has neither gone astray nor amiss. Nor does he speak out of his own desire. It is just a revelation that is revealed (to him).

SURAH AL-NAJM, VERSES: 1-4

The tafsīr of Ibn Abbas describes an occasion when Rasulullah(s) was sitting amongst his companions and a falling star caught everyone's attention. Rasulullah(s) immediately stated:

> "In whosoever's house direction the star will fall, he will be the successor after me."

It was witnessed by many: the star fell in the direction of Imam Ali's(as) house.

In other narrations, Muhammad ibn al-Abbas reports from multiple chains, that Imam Sadiq(as) said, "Rasulullah(s) was present in the company of some men from Quraysh when he(s) said, 'I am the master of mankind, and Ali(as) is the master of the believers. O God! Be the friend of whoever is Ali's friend and the enemy of whoever is Ali's enemy.' Thereupon a man declared, 'By God, he doesn't cease from praising his cousin ever.'"

That is when Allah revealed these verses, informing that Rasulullah(s) never speaks of his own, but rather only delivers what Allah commands.

Sources: *The Luminous Flashes* (842nd Name)

Instruction about the Announcement

يَا أَيُّهَا الرَّسُولُ بَلِّغْ مَا أُنزِلَ إِلَيْكَ مِن رَّبِّكَ ۖ وَإِن لَّمْ تَفْعَلْ فَمَا بَلَّغْتَ رِسَالَتَهُ ۚ وَاللَّهُ يَعْصِمُكَ مِنَ النَّاسِ ۗ إِنَّ اللَّهَ لَا يَهْدِي الْقَوْمَ الْكَافِرِينَ

O Apostle! Communicate that which has been sent down to you from your Lord, and if you do not, you will not have communicated His message, and Allah shall protect you from the people. Indeed Allah does not guide the faithless lot.

SURAH AL-MA'IDAH, VERSE: 67

On numerous occasions Rasulullah(s) had informed people about the guardianship of Imam Ali(as). Unfortunately, it wasn't understood amongst many. Hence when Rasulullah(s) was returning from his last Hajj, Allah commanded him to explain Ali's guardianship just as he had explained the prayers, fasting, hajj and zakat. Rasulullah(s) was worried that people would not believe him and would potentially abandon their faith.

> This verse strengthened Rasulullah(s) so he moved forward to fulfill the order.

Sources: *The Luminous Flashes* (188th Name), *Al-Burhan*, vol.1, pp.488-491

Announcement of Imam Ali's (as) Succession

الْيَوْمَ أَكْمَلْتُ لَكُمْ دِينَكُمْ وَأَتْمَمْتُ عَلَيْكُمْ نِعْمَتِي وَرَضِيتُ لَكُمُ الْإِسْلَامَ دِينًا

Today I have perfected your religion for you and I have completed My blessing upon you, and I have approved Islam as your religion.

SURAH AL-MA'IDAH, VERSE: 3

Rasulullah(s) gathered everyone at the point of Ghadir Khumm and directed a few of his companions to construct a pulpit out of saddles so that he could deliver a sermon. In this sermon not only did Rasulullah(s) explain about the pillars and practices of Islam but he also informed of the coming of the twelve Imams. He then took Imam Ali(as) upon the pulpit, raised his arms in front of hundreds of thousands of people and pronounced Imam Ali(as) the wali (leader) of the believers. As he raised Imam Ali's hands he uttered the following words:

For whomsoever I am master*, then this Ali(as) is his master.*

As soon as he made the announcement Gabriel(as) descended with this verse. The event was recorded in history as the *Hadith Al-Ghadir*.

*The term *master* here means Divinely appointed authority.

COMPLETION OF BLESSINGS
Some facts about this verse

REVEALED ON
18th of Dul al-Hijjah, 10 AH

WHERE
Near a pond called "Ghadir Khumm" which is located on the road from Mecca to Madina. It is 4 km away from Juhfa. Juhfa is one of the five Miqats for pilgrims performing Hajj. Due to the water supply and the shade of a few trees, Ghadir Khumm was a stopping place for caravans.

ATTENDEES
Over 100,000 Muslims

SIGNIFICANCE OF 18TH DUL AL HIJJAH AFTER THIS EVENT
This day is celebrated as "Eid al Ghadir" amongst Shia Muslims every year. This Eid is also known as the "Greatest Eid of God", as Rasulullah(s) delivered the final instruction to the ummah, which was the establishment of *Imamat* (the system of Divinely appointed guides).

Reflections

Use this space to pen down your precious thoughts.

Generosity

Generosity is to give the most desired things, and be hospitable to the seeker.

—ALI IBN ABI TALIB (AS)

GENEROSITY

Just as the father caters to the needs of his children and prefers their wishes over his own, a generous person is always willing to serve others with all he has. At times, he is able to identify the needy amongst the society and cater to their needs. Throughout his life, Imam Ali(as) spent his wealth, time and services for the betterment of his community, especially the orphans. It is noted in history that Imam Ali(as) spent all of his share from the spoils of Khaybar on the orphans and widows of the community. This wasn't an isolated event. He always preferred to disperse his gains from the spoils of war amongst the poor. Imam Ali(as) established his engagement with the orphans during the life of Rasulullah(s), and it only grew stronger with time. His reported conduct with the orphans reminds us that money isn't the only way to help others; one can be generous with his time, conduct and moral support. The Holy Qur'an remembers Imam Ali(as) as the one who is fearless and always ready to serve others in the way of Allah.

Imam Ali's Charity

الَّذِينَ يُنفِقُونَ أَمْوَالَهُم بِاللَّيْلِ وَالنَّهَارِ سِرًّا وَعَلَانِيَةً فَلَهُمْ أَجْرُهُمْ عِندَ رَبِّهِمْ وَلَا خَوْفٌ عَلَيْهِمْ وَلَا هُمْ يَحْزَنُونَ

Those who spend their wealth [in Allah's way] by night and by day, secretly and publicly– they will have their reward with their Lord. And no fear will there be concerning them, nor will they grieve.

SURAH AL-BAQARAH, VERSE: 274

It is narrated by Shaykh Al Mufid in *Al-Ikhtisas* and also by Abu Ishaq:

Once Rasulullah(s) asked Imam Ali(as): "O Ali! What did you do at night?"

He said: "I had four dirhams, so I gave them to charity: one by night, one by day, one secretly and one openly."

Rasulullah(s) further inquired: "What made you do that?"

Imam Ali(as) replied: "To fulfill Allah's promise." Rasulullah(s) then stated that Allah has revealed this verse in the praise of Ali(as).

Source: *The Luminous Flashes* (61st Name)

Voluntary Donor

الَّذِينَ يَلْمِزُونَ الْمُطَّوِّعِينَ مِنَ الْمُؤْمِنِينَ فِي الصَّدَقَاتِ وَالَّذِينَ لَا يَجِدُونَ إِلَّا جُهْدَهُمْ فَيَسْخَرُونَ مِنْهُمْ سَخِرَ اللَّهُ مِنْهُمْ وَلَهُمْ عَذَابٌ أَلِيمٌ

Those who criticize the contributors among the believers concerning [their] charities and [criticize] the ones who find nothing [to spend] except their effort, so they ridicule them—Allah will ridicule them, and they will have a painful punishment.

SURAH AT-TAWBAH, VERSE: 79

Abu al-Jarud narrates from Imam Jafar Sadiq(as), "Once Imam Ali(as) went and hired himself out to fetch water buckets in return for dates. He collected several dates and brought them to Rasulullah(s). As Imam Ali(as) was entering, Abd al Rahman ibn Awf was standing by the door. He pointed towards Ali(as) and slandered him. This verse was revealed along with the following one. It states that Allah will not forgive the evildoers even if Rasulullah(s) was to plead for their forgiveness seventy times."

30 | *The Father of Orphans*   Sources: *The Luminous Flashes* (250th Name), *Al-'Ayyashi*, vol.2, p.101

Maintainer of Zakat

وَالَّذِينَ هُمْ لِلزَّكَاةِ فَاعِلُونَ

And those who carry out their duty of zakat.

SURAH AL-MUMINOON, VERSE:4

The commentary of *Al-Burhan* provides an in-depth analysis of the first few verses of this Surah. It is reported that these verses were specifically revealed in praise of the Ahlul Bayt(as). They describe the characteristics of mumineen. Imam Ali(as) personified these traits and was referred to as Amirul Momineen(as). Amongst those characteristics is the maintenance of zakat (religious tax). Under his rulership, Imam Ali(as) established a well-defined system for the distribution of zakat. The income collected under this category was spent amongst the poor, orphans and widows in the form of pensions and stipends. Zakat was also used to support the Hajis (pilgrims) and to free slaves.

SURAH AL-MUMINOON

Imam Ali(as) recited the first 11 verses of this surah when he met Rasulullah(s) after his birth. Rasulullah(s) then exclaimed, "O Ali! Indeed Momineen will gain salvation through you."

Source: *The Luminous Flashes* (466th Name)

Generosity | 31

The One Whose Charity is Accepted

> رِجَالٌ لَّا تُلْهِيهِمْ تِجَارَةٌ وَلَا بَيْعٌ عَن ذِكْرِ اللَّهِ وَإِقَامِ الصَّلَاةِ وَإِيتَاءِ الزَّكَاةِ
>
> By men whom neither trade nor bargaining distracts from the remembrance of Allah and the maintenance of prayer and the giving of zakat.
>
> SURAH AN NOOR, VERSE: 37

In the commentary of this verse, Ibn Abbas narrates once Rasulullah(s) gave Imam Ali(as) 300 dinars, which he had received as a gift. Imam Ali(as) took the money and made an intention to give it out as charity in a way that Allah would accept it. At night, he completed his prayers with Rasulullah(s), took a hundred dinars out, and left the mosque. On his way, he met a needy woman and gave her the money. In the morning, he heard people talking about his charity claiming that he had given money to a corrupt woman. He became heartbroken upon hearing this, and made the intention for his next round of charity.

The following night after prayers, he left the mosque to hand out more money, met a man and gave him a hundred dinars. The next morning he found the people of Medina saying, "Ali gave charity to a thief." This caused Imam Ali(as) great sorrow. He then made the intention to hand out his last hundred dinars as a charity in the best possible manner.

That night after leaving the mosque, he saw a man and thereupon he gave him the last hundred dinars. In the morning, he heard the people of Medina saying, "Last night Ali(as) gave charity to a rich man." Once again, the news gave him great sorrow so he visited

Rasulullah(s) and told him the story. Rasulullah(s) said, "O Ali(as)! Gabriel(as) says to you, 'Allah has accepted your charity and purified your acts.'"

Rasulullah(s) then revealed the backstory of Imam Ali's(as) charities, "The charity you gave to the woman became the source of earning for her. She also intends to get married with this money. Your second charity went to a thief, who has since repented and intends to use this money for a business. The last charity went to a rich man who hadn't paid alms in many years. Your charity made him ashamed and he said: 'How miserly I am! This is Ali ibn Abi Talib (as) who gave away a hundred dinars to me while he has nothing, whereas I am a rich man who has not paid his obligatory alms!' So he has calculated his alms and put it aside for distribution."

It was for these reasons Allah revealed this verse in praise of Imam Ali's(as) charity.

Source: duas.org

Giver of Charity

وَالْمُتَصَدِّقِينَ وَالْمُتَصَدِّقَاتِ...

The men and women who give in charity.

SURAH AL-AHZAAB, VERSE: 35

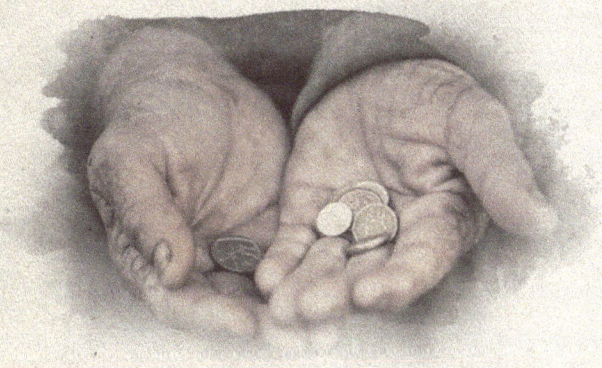

This verse was revealed along with the **verse of purification (33:33)**. It showcases some of the titles with which Allah has remembered the Ahlul Bayt(as). As a member of the household of Rasulullah(s), Imam Ali(as) carries all of those noble titles. Being amongst the charity givers denotes that Allah recognises and accepts all of his charities.

Source: *The Luminous Flashes* (616th-625th Names)

Generosity | 33

Reflections

Use this space to pen down your precious thoughts.

_____
_____
_____
_____
_____
_____
_____
_____
_____
_____
_____
_____
_____
_____

Devotion

Do not betray anyone who places his trust in you, even if he betrays you, and do not disclose his secrets, even if he discloses yours.

—ALI IBN ABI TALIB (AS)

DEVOTION

Devotion is a trait by which one demonstrates their loyalty, love and steadfastness through action. Over the course of his entire life, Imam Ali(as) proved himself to be the most devoted servant of Allah and His Messenger(s). His actions were a true reflection of his utmost belief in the Almighty. Whether it was playing with orphans until they laughed, being present as a fierce soldier on the battlefield, sleeping on the bed of Rasulullah(s) or fulfilling the needs of the underprivileged, he presented his selfless services in every way possible to attain the pleasure of Allah. His religious devotion helped him develop a trustful and close relationship with orphans. As a man of great integrity and honor he inculcated great moral values in the orphans of his community.

While caring for orphans, Imam Ali's(as) goal was always to serve the Creator and to remain obedient to Him under all circumstances. The verses in this section reveal his love for the Almighty in times of trial as well as his utmost devotion towards Rasulullah(s) on every occasion.

Remembering Allah in Times of Affliction

الَّذِينَ إِذَا أَصَابَتْهُم مُّصِيبَةٌ قَالُوا إِنَّا لِلَّهِ وَإِنَّا إِلَيْهِ رَاجِعُونَ

Those who, when an affliction visits them say, "Indeed we belong to Allah and to Him do we indeed return."

SURAH AL-BAQARA, VERSE: 156

The famous part of this verse was first uttered by Imam Ali(as) when he heard about the demise of Hazrat Hamza(as) in the battle of Uhud. It is also reported in *al-Manaqib* by Ibn Shahr that when Rasulullah(s) announced the death of Jafar ibn Abi Talib in the battle of Mu'tah, Imam Ali(as) expressed his sadness about the loss of his brother by uttering these same words. Allah loved this servitude of Ali(as) so much that it was revealed as a verse in the Holy Qur'an. Since then, it has become a common practice amongst Muslims to recite this verse upon hearing any tragic news.

Source: *The Luminous Flashes* (45th -48th Name)

Receiver of Allah's Blessings

أُولَٰئِكَ عَلَيْهِمْ صَلَوَاتٌ مِّن رَّبِّهِمْ وَرَحْمَةٌ ۖ وَأُولَٰئِكَ هُمُ الْمُهْتَدُونَ

It is they who receive the blessings of their Lord and His mercy, and it is they who are the rightly guided.

SURAH AL-BAQARA, VERSE: 157

This verse, which is connected to the previous one, indicates that Imam Ali(as) became the receiver of Allah's blessings due to his obedience towards the Almighty. The context of this verse became one of the reasons for sending Salawat on the Holy Prophet(s) and his family in our Salah.

Attaining Allah's Pleasure on the Night of Hijrah

وَمِنَ النَّاسِ مَن يَشْرِي نَفْسَهُ ابْتِغَاءَ مَرْضَاتِ اللَّهِ ۗ وَاللَّهُ رَءُوفٌ بِالْعِبَادِ

And among the people is he who sells his soul seeking the pleasure of Allah, and Allah is most kind to (His) servants.

SURAH AL-BAQARA, VERSE: 207

A number of traditions indicate that this verse was revealed in honour of Imam Ali(as) when he slept in the bed of Rasulullah(s) on the night of Hijrah (migration). This selfless act of Imam Ali(as) saved Rasulullah's(s) life from the idolaters of Makkah. Therefore Allah recognised and praised Imam Ali's(as) action in this verse.

In other narrations, it is also reported by Abu Dharr(ra) that a companion formed a committee of Imam Ali(as) and a few others, to select a successor. Each candidate was asked to mention their achievements as a means to ease the selection process. Imam Ali(as) mentioned many of his feats and quoted the above verse as evidence in support of his outstanding achievements and proved that he was the rightful successor of the Holy Prophet(s).

Source: *The Luminous Flashes* (56th Name)

The Soul of Rasulullah (s)

> فَمَنْ حَاجَّكَ فِيهِ مِنْ بَعْدِ مَا جَاءَكَ مِنَ الْعِلْمِ فَقُلْ تَعَالَوْا نَدْعُ أَبْنَاءَنَا وَأَبْنَاءَكُمْ وَنِسَاءَنَا وَنِسَاءَكُمْ وَأَنفُسَنَا وَأَنفُسَكُمْ ثُمَّ نَبْتَهِلْ فَنَجْعَل لَّعْنَتَ اللَّهِ عَلَى الْكَاذِبِينَ.
>
> Then whoever argues with you about it after [this] knowledge has come to you say: Come, let us call our sons and your sons, our women and your women, OURSELVES and yourselves, then supplicate earnestly [together] and invoke the curse of Allah upon the liars [among us].
>
> SURAH AAL-IMRAN, VERSE: 61

In the event of Mubahala, Allah instructed Rasulullah(s) to gather the sons, women, and someone equal to him in character, justice, knowledge and stature. For the completion of Allah's command Rasulullah(s) brought the Ahlul Bayt(as). Amongst the Ahlul Bayt(as) Imam Hasan(as) and Imam Hussain(as) were representing his sons, Syeda Fatima(sa) his women and Imam Ali(as) was brought as an extension of his personality, i.e he was the 'soul' of Rasulullah(s). Upon witnessing the light on the faces of Rasulullah(s) and his household, the Christian delegation from Najran retreated and made peace with them in return for a tribute.

> By God, I see the faces which, if they pray to God for mountains to move from their places, the mountains will immediately move!
>
> — CHRISTIAN DELEGATE AT MUBAHALA

MUBAHALA
Some facts about the Mubahala

MEANING OF 'MUBAHALA'
Praying to Allah to withdraw His mercy from one who lies or engages in falsehood.

DATE OF MUBAHALA
24 Dhu al-Hijjah, 10 AH

ATTENDEES
Rasulullah(s) with Ahlul Bayt(as) & Christian delegation from Najran

THE SUBJECT OF DISCUSSION
To prove whether Jesus is God or a SERVANT of God.

RESULT
The Christain delegation surrendered giving victory to Rasulullah(s) and the Ahlul Bayt(as).

In the remembrance of this remarkable victory over the Christians, Shia Muslims celebrate Eid al-Mubahala.

Being Amongst The Virtuous

وَسَنَجْزِي الشَّاكِرِينَ ﴿١٤٥﴾ وَكَأَيِّن مِّن نَّبِيٍّ قَاتَلَ مَعَهُ رِبِّيُّونَ كَثِيرٌ فَمَا وَهَنُوا لِمَا أَصَابَهُمْ فِي سَبِيلِ اللَّهِ وَمَا ضَعُفُوا وَمَا اسْتَكَانُوا وَاللَّهُ يُحِبُّ الصَّابِرِينَ ﴿١٤٦﴾ وَمَا كَانَ قَوْلَهُمْ إِلَّا أَن قَالُوا رَبَّنَا اغْفِرْ لَنَا ذُنُوبَنَا وَإِسْرَافَنَا فِي أَمْرِنَا وَثَبِّتْ أَقْدَامَنَا وَانصُرْنَا عَلَى الْقَوْمِ الْكَافِرِينَ ﴿١٤٧﴾ فَآتَاهُمُ اللَّهُ ثَوَابَ الدُّنْيَا وَحُسْنَ ثَوَابِ الْآخِرَةِ وَاللَّهُ يُحِبُّ الْمُحْسِنِينَ ﴿١٤٨﴾

And we will reward the grateful. How many a prophet there has been with whom a multitude of lordly men fought. They did not falter for what befell them in the way of Allah, neither did they weaken, nor did they abase themselves; and Allah loves the steadfast. All that they said was: Our Lord, forgive us our sins and our excesses in our affairs, and make our feet firm, and help us against the disbelieving folk. So Allah gave them the reward of this world and the good reward of the Hereafter, and Allah loves the virtuous.

SURAH AAL-IMRAN, VERSES: 145-148

These verses were revealed in the praise of Imam Ali(as) discussing his demeanor in the battle of Uhud. He suffered 80 wounds during the fight. Despite these grave injuries, he remained valiant on the battlefield. When Rasulullah(s) saw him in this state he wept and said, "Indeed God is entitled to reward a man who is afflicted by this for His sake." Imam Ali(as) replied:

> "Praise belongs to God, who has not seen me turning my tracks from you nor running away. You are as dear to me as my own father and mother! Why was I deprived of martyrdom?"

Rasulullah(s) informed him about Abu Sufyan's threat at Hamra' al-Asad and sent him with a few companions to ward off the enemy.

Trusting in the Power of Allah

الَّذِينَ قَالَ لَهُمُ النَّاسُ إِنَّ النَّاسَ قَدْ جَمَعُوا لَكُمْ فَاخْشَوْهُمْ فَزَادَهُمْ إِيمَانًا وَقَالُوا حَسْبُنَا اللَّهُ وَنِعْمَ الْوَكِيلُ

Those to whom the people said, "All the people have gathered against you, so fear them." That only increased them in faith and they said, "Allah is sufficient for us and He is an excellent trustee."

SURAH AAL-IMRAN, VERSE: 173

When Rasulullah(s) returned to Madina after the battle of Uhud, Allah ordered him to follow Abu Sufyan as he was planning to exterminate Muslims completely after weakening them at Uhud. Rasulullah(s) sent a few of his special companions with Imam Ali(as) to camp out in Hamra Al-Asad and frighten the Meccans. En route, Imam Ali(as) and his companions encountered Nuaym ibn Masud who tried to convince them not to fight with the Meccans by exaggerating their numbers. Imam Ali(as) showed his utmost trust by saying **"Allah is sufficient for us, and He is an excellent trustee."** Allah loved this gesture so much that He revealed this verse in praise of him.

Allah is sufficient for us, and He is an excellent trustee.

Sources: *The Luminous Flashes* (111th -115th Name), *Al-'Ayyashi*, vol.1, p.206

The One Who is Loved by Allah

فَسَوْفَ يَأْتِي اللَّهُ بِقَوْمٍ يُحِبُّهُمْ وَيُحِبُّونَهُ أَذِلَّةٍ عَلَى الْمُؤْمِنِينَ أَعِزَّةٍ عَلَى الْكَافِرِينَ يُجَاهِدُونَ فِي سَبِيلِ اللَّهِ وَلَا يَخَافُونَ لَوْمَةَ لَائِمٍ

Allah will soon bring a people whom He loves and who love Him, {who will be} humble towards the faithful, stern towards the faithless, waging jihad in the way of Allah, not fearing the blame of any blamer.

SURAH AL-MAI'DAH, VERSE: 54

The tafsīr of this verse reveals the qualities which are attained by none other than Imam Ali(as). Rasulullah(s) in the battle of "Khaybar" used the same wording for him:

"Tomorrow, I will hand over the flag of the Islamic army to a person who is brave and who does not flee from the battlefield. That is one who is absolutely courageous and never bolts from the field. One who loves Allah and the Messenger and Allah and the Messenger love him. He will not return till Allah grants victory at his hands."

In *Nahj al-Bayan* by al-Shaybani, it is reported from Imam al-Baqir(as) and al-Sadiq(as) that this verse was revealed concerning Ameeriul Momineen(as).

Source: *The Luminous Flashes* (185th Name)

Devotion

Reflections

Use this space to pen down your precious thoughts.

_____

_____

_____

_____

_____

_____

_____

_____

_____

_____

_____

_____

_____

Kindness

The best of the manners of mankind is that of kindness.

—ALI IBN ABI TALIB (AS)

KINDNESS

Kindness reflects the compassion, love and mercy of a person. A father's kindness towards his kids shapes their confidence and encourages them to take challenges in their lives. His kindness and love diminishes their fears and helps them create a positive and respected image in society. Imam Ali(as)—who was brought up by Rasulullah(s)—witnessed the Prophet's(s) utmost affection and love for everyone. In his will to Imam Ali(as), Rasulullah(s) said:

"O Ali, for those who pass their hands on an orphan's head as a sign of mercy, God will give them illumination for every single hair (of that head) on the Day of Resurrection."[1]

While walking in those footsteps, Imam Ali(as) gave special attention and care to the orphans and the impoverished. If he saw an orphan crying in the street, he would stop whatever he was doing to console the child. Through his kindness, love and joyousness, Imam Ali(as) drew the orphans nearer to himself. He made sure not only to feed their hunger but to remain playful with them, lifting their self-esteem. Imam Ali(as) taught his followers to take special care of the orphans of the martyrs. He used to say, "Their fathers were martyred in jihad for the sake of Islam and they have rights on you. Make their souls pleased with you by cheering up their children and looking after them." In the Holy Qur'an, Allah remembers Imam Ali(as) amongst those who treat the orphans and poor with kindness and prefer others in need over themselves.

---

1   Ibid., vol. 74, p. 60.

Giving Charity in Difficult Times

وَالَّذِينَ تَبَوَّءُوا الدَّارَ وَالْإِيمَانَ مِن قَبْلِهِمْ يُحِبُّونَ مَنْ هَاجَرَ إِلَيْهِمْ وَلَا يَجِدُونَ فِي صُدُورِهِمْ حَاجَةً مِّمَّا أُوتُوا وَيُؤْثِرُونَ عَلَىٰ أَنفُسِهِمْ وَلَوْ كَانَ بِهِمْ خَصَاصَةٌ

And [also for] those who were settled in al-Madinah and [adopted] the faith before them. They love those who migrated to them and find not any want in their breasts of what the immigrants were given but give [them] preference over themselves, even though poverty be their own lot.

SURAH AL-HASHR, VERSE: 9

This verse indicates the time when Imam Ali(as) & Syeda Fatimah(sa) were going through some rough times because of their finances. Syeda Fatimah(sa) requested Imam Ali(as) to visit Rasulullah(s) for a loan. He came to Rasulullah(s) who gave him a dinar and said, "O Ali! Go and purchase food for your family."

As Imam Ali(as) went forth he encountered al-Miqdad ibn al Aswad(ra) who was out in the market and was looking distressed. Ameer ul Momineen(as) asked Miqdad(ra) about his condition to which he reluctantly responded that he has no money to purchase food for his kids. Imam Ali(as) gave his dinar to him and went to the mosque. After spending some time there when he returned home, he found Rasulullah(s) waiting for him. He asked him "O Ali! What did you do?" Imam Ali(as) explained how he had helped al-Miqdad(ra). To which Rasulullah(s) replied "Gabriel had informed me about your meeting. Allah had revealed these verses in your praise and had also sent delicious food for your family from the heavens."

Kindness | 49

The Helper of Poor and Orphans

وَيُطْعِمُونَ الطَّعَامَ عَلَىٰ حُبِّهِ مِسْكِينًا وَيَتِيمًا وَأَسِيرًا

For the love of Him, they feed the needy, the orphans and the prisoner.

SURAH AL-INSAAN, VERSE: 8

This surah is also remembered as Surah Ad-Dahar. It is reported that once Imam Hasan(as) and Imam Hussain(as) fell ill. When Rasulullah(s) visited them, he suggested Imam Ali(as) and Syeda Fatimah(sa) make a nadhr[2] for their recovery. They took his advice and vowed to keep three fasts.

After a few days when the children had recovered, the Ahlul Bayt(as) fulfilled their vows and began their fasting. On the first day, at the time of iftar when Imam Ali(as) and his family were about to break their fast, a beggar came to the door requesting some food. Imam Ali(as), his family and their maid Lady Fizza gave all of their food away to help the needy.

2   Nadhr: It is a vow in which that a person makes it obligatory upon himself to do some good actions for the sake of God or abandons some bad actions for the sake of God

They encountered a similar situation the next day and served an orphan from their food. On the last day of fasting, the Ahlul Bayt(as) satiated the hunger of a slave and remained patient on breaking their fast with just water. The next morning Imam Ali(as) brought Al-Hasnain(as) to visit Rasulullah(s). Imam Hasan(as) and Imam Hussain(as) advanced towards the Messenger of Allah(s), trembling out of extreme hunger. Rasulullah(s) caught their sight and said, "O Abu al Hasan, it gives me extreme sorrow to see you all in this condition." Then he rose up and advanced to their house where he found Syeda Fatimah(sa) in a state of extreme weakness. Rasulullah(s) was beginning to get worried when Gabriel(as) descended and said:

> "O Messenger of Allah, congratulations! Allah has sent this surah in praise of the actions of your Ahlul Bayt(as)"

and he recited "Indeed the righteous will drink from a cup [of wine] whose mixture is of Kafur." (76:5)

Source: *The Luminous Flashes* (998th Name)

The One Who is Remembered as Kindness

إِنَّ اللَّهَ يَأْمُرُ بِالْعَدْلِ وَالْإِحْسَانِ

Indeed Allah commands justice and kindness...

SURAH AL-NAHL, VERSE: 90

Ali ibn Ibrahim reports from the chain of narrations leading to Imam Baqir(as), that "justice" in this verse refers to bearing testimony that there is no god but God and that Muhammad(s) is the Messenger of God, and "kindness" refers to the friendship of the Commander of the faithful(as).

Source: *The Luminous Flashes* (338th Name)

Reflections

Use this space to pen down your precious thoughts.

Spirituality

O Allah! I do not worship you for fear of punishment or in hope of reward; rather, I know you worthy of worshipping so I worship you.[3]

—ALI IBN ABI TALIB (AS)

[3] *Biharul Anwar*, Vol 41, p. 14

SPIRITUALITY

The spirituality of a person reflects their individual connection with the Divine. This particular relationship between God and His servant enables the person to grow in spiritual rank. Imam Ali's (as) immense worship and servitude qualified him to attain such levels of spirituality that Allah bestowed special favors and blessings upon him. Imam Sajjad (as) was once reading a book in which Imam Ali's (as) worship was recorded. He put the book down and said, **"Who can worship like Ali Ibn Abi Talib (as)?"**[4]

As the Father of orphans, Imam Ali (as) was carefully building, nurturing and shielding the spiritual connection of orphans with the Almighty. His piety and sincerity made him play a distinctive role in shaping the personalities of those orphans. He cherished his time with them, playfully teaching those who were suffering due to the absence of a fatherly figure in their lives.

The verses in this section on spirituality will explore a few of the unique favors and titles the Almighty gave to Imam Ali (as) for being His true servant.

---

[4] *Biharul Anwar*, Vol 41, p. 17

Acceptance of Islam

وَالَّذِي جَاءَ بِالصِّدْقِ وَصَدَّقَ بِهِ ۙ أُولَٰئِكَ هُمُ الْمُتَّقُونَ...

He who brings the truth and he who confirms it—it is they who are the God-wary.

SURAH AZ-ZUMAR, VERSE: 33

This verse refers to the time when Rasulullah(s) introduced the religion of Islam to his relatives and invited them to accept it. Imam Ali(as) was the only one to outwardly accept the faith and testify to Rasulullah's(s) Prophethood. The Prophet(s) accepted his testimony and announced, "Ali(as) will be my inheritor and deputy."

It is important to understand that all the Prophets(s) and Imams(as) believe in the concept of tawhid—oneness of Allah—from birth; but they only declare it to others by the will of Allah in its due time.

"The first among you to meet me at the pond (in heaven) is the first among you to embrace Islam—that is Ali..." [5]

— PROPHET MUHAMMAD (S)

---

5 Pg. 35 of *Seerat al-A'immah* by Sh. Jafar Subhani

The Rope of Allah

وَاعْتَصِمُوا بِحَبْلِ اللَّهِ جَمِيعًا وَلَا تَفَرَّقُوا

And hold firmly to the rope of Allah all together and do not become divided.

SURAH AAL-IMRAN, VERSE: 103

Once, Rasulullah(s) was sitting in the mosque along with his companions when a man approached him. He mentioned the above verse and asked, "O Messenger of God! So what is this rope which God has commanded us to hold fast and not to separate from?" Rasulullah(s) pondered for some time and then pointed towards Imam Ali(as) while saying

"This is the rope of God. Whoever holds fast to it will be protected from going astray in this world and the hereafter."

It is also reported from Shaykh Al Tusi in his book *Al-Amali*, that Imam Jafar Sadiq(as) had said, "We the Ahlul Bayt(as) are the rope of Allah to which He has commanded you to hold firmly."

Sources: *The Luminous Flashes* (81st Name), *Al-Burhan*, vol.1, pp. 305-306.

Allah's Grace

وَلَوْلَا فَضْلُ اللَّهِ عَلَيْكُمْ وَرَحْمَتُهُ لَاتَّبَعْتُمُ الشَّيْطَانَ إِلَّا قَلِيلًا

And were it not for Allah's grace upon you and His mercy, you would have surely followed Satan, {all} except a few.

SURAH AN-NISA, VERSE: 83

It is reported from Al-'Ayyashi that Allah's "mercy" is in reference to the Messenger of Allah(s) and His "grace" to that of Ali Ibn Abi Talib(as). The reverse meaning is also reported by the same narrator. Al-'Ayyashi once reported the meaning of this verse from the chains of narrations leading back to Imam Muhammad Baqir(as) that:

Allah's "grace" is His messenger and His "mercy" is the friendship of the Imams (as).

Sources: *The Luminous Flashes* (170th Name), *Al-Burhan*, vol.1, p.398; and *Al-'Ayyashi*, vol.1, pp.260-261

Knower of Secrets

Ha, Meem

SURAH ASH-SHURA, VERSE: 1

Ibn Abbas's tafsir for this verse indicates that the power of these two Huruf Al Muqaṭṭaʿāt (mysterious letters) coupled with Imam Ali's(as) knowledge of them revealed the names of past, present and future nations and secrets about their crimes. Imam's(as) immense and hidden knowledge on such matters became a source of guidance for the people around him.

The Straight Path

وَأَنَّ هَٰذَا صِرَاطِي مُسْتَقِيمًا فَاتَّبِعُوهُ وَلَا تَتَّبِعُوا السُّبُلَ فَتَفَرَّقَ بِكُمْ عَن سَبِيلِهِ

This indeed is *My straight path,* so follow it, and do not follow (other) ways, for they will separate you from His way.

SURAH AL-ANAAM, VERSE: 153

It has been narrated by Jabir ibn Abdullah that once Rasulullah(s) was sitting amongst his companions when he pointed towards Imam Ali(as) and said:

"This is a straight path, so follow it."

Ibrahim al Thaqafi also reported that the "straight path" in this verse is Ali ibn Abi Talib(as). He mentioned the background of the verse on the authority of Abu Buraydah that he said, "Rasulullah(s) had said 'Surely this is my straight path, so follow it, and do not follow other ways, lest you should be parted from His way. I asked Allah to appoint it for Ali and He did.'"

Sources: *The Luminous Flashes* (198th Name), *Al-Burhan*, vol.1, p.563

A Caller on the Day of Judgement

فَأَذَّنَ مُؤَذِّنٌ بَيْنَهُمْ أَن لَّعْنَةُ اللَّهِ عَلَى الظَّالِمِينَ

Then a caller will announce in their midst, "May Allah's curse be on the wrongdoers!

SURAH AL-A'RAF, VERSE: 44

Jabir al Ju'fi narrates from Imam Muhammad Baqir(as): Once Imam Ali(as) was informed that Muawiyah had abused him and had killed his companions. So he stood and delivered a sermon. In that sermon, Imam Ali(as) mentioned this verse and said:

"I am the caller in this world and the hereafter."

Abu Salih ibn Abbas is reported to have said, "In the Qur'an, Imam Ali(as) has names of which people have no knowledge of, and amongst them is this verse." Imam Ali(as) will cry on the Day of Judgement:

"The curse of Allah is on those who deny my friendship and deem light my claim."

> "I am the caller in this world and the hereafter."
>
> —IMAM ALI (AS)

Sources: *The Luminous Flashes* (206th Name), *Al-Burhan*, vol.2, p.17.

Allah's Light

الَّذِينَ يَتَّبِعُونَ الرَّسُولَ النَّبِيَّ الْأُمِّيَّ الَّذِي يَجِدُونَهُ مَكْتُوبًا عِندَهُمْ فِي التَّوْرَاةِ وَالْإِنجِيلِ......فَالَّذِينَ آمَنُوا بِهِ وَعَزَّرُوهُ وَنَصَرُوهُ وَاتَّبَعُوا النُّورَ الَّذِي أُنزِلَ مَعَهُ ۙ أُولَٰئِكَ هُمُ الْمُفْلِحُونَ ۞

Those who follow the Apostle, the untaught Prophet, whom they find inscribed in the Torah and the Gospel...Those who believe in him, honor him, help him and follow the light that has been sent down with him; they are the felicitous.

SURAH AN-NISA, VERSE: 83

Ahmad ibn Muhammad narrates from Imam Baqir(as) that Rasulullah(s), his executor Imam Ali(as) and al-Qaim(as) are the ones who are mentioned in Torah and Gospel.

It is stated by Al-Ayyashi on the authority of Imam Baqir(as) that Imam Ali(as) is referred to as the "Light that has been sent down with Rasulullah(s)".

> Ali and I are of the same light.
>
> —PROPHET MUHAMMAD (S)

The Father of Orphans

Source: *The Luminous Flashes* (210th Name)

The Divider of Heaven and Hell

وَبَيْنَهُمَا حِجَابٌ ۚ وَعَلَى الْأَعْرَافِ رِجَالٌ يَعْرِفُونَ كُلًّا بِسِيمَاهُمْ ۚ وَنَادَوْا أَصْحَابَ الْجَنَّةِ أَنْ سَلَامٌ عَلَيْكُمْ لَمْ يَدْخُلُوهَا وَهُمْ يَطْمَعُونَ

There will be a veil between them. And on the elevations will be certain men who recognize each of them by their mark. They will call out to the inhabitants of paradise, "Peace be to you!" They will not have entered it, though they would be eager to do so.

SURAH AL-A'RAF, VERSE: 46

A'raf is a place between hell and heaven where those who will have equal amounts of good and bad deeds will be placed. It is mentioned in many traditions that on the day of judgement Imam Ali(as) will be standing on an elevation in A'raf along with other men. They will recognize their friends from the light emitting from their faces, and will bring them towards Heaven. However, their enemies will have a dark mark on their faces by which Imam Ali(as) will recognize them as well.

Asbagh ibn Nubatah was once sitting with the Commander of the Faithful(as) when a man asked him about this verse. Imam Ali(as) replied,

"We are the Ramparts. We know our helpers by their mark. On the day of judgement we will be made to stand up between the Garden and the Fire. No one will enter the Garden except him who knows us and whom we know, and no one will enter the Fire except him who rejects us and whom we reject."

Source: *The Luminous Flashes* (207th Name)

Purifier For Hearts

وَيُنَزِّلُ عَلَيْكُم مِّنَ السَّمَاءِ مَاءً لِّيُطَهِّرَكُم بِهِ وَيُذْهِبَ عَنكُمْ رِجْزَ الشَّيْطَانِ...

And He sent down water from the sky to purify you with it, and repel from you the defilement of Satan.

SURAH AL-ANFAAL, VERSE: 11

Al-A'yashi reports that Jabir once asked Imam Jafar Sadiq(as) the inward meaning of this verse. The Imam replied, "The sky, inwardly, is Rasulullah(s) and the water is Ali(as). Allah has made Ali(as) from Rasulullah(s). So Allah purifies the heart, repels defilement of Satan, and strengthens the heart of whoever befriends Ali(as)."

"The Almighty protects the heart of the believer by Ali(as), so he remains firm towards his friendship."

Sources: *The Luminous Flashes* (222th-225th Name); *Al-'Ayyashi*, vol.2, p.50; & *Al-Burhan*, vol.2, p.69.

Allah's Help

وَإِن يُرِيدُوا أَن يَخْدَعُوكَ فَإِنَّ حَسْبَكَ اللَّهُ ۚ هُوَ الَّذِي أَيَّدَكَ بِنَصْرِهِ وَبِالْمُؤْمِنِينَ

But if they desire to deceive you, Allah is indeed sufficient for you. It is He who strengthened you *with His help* and with the means of the faithful.

SURAH AL-ANFAAL, VERSE: 62

Ibn Asker narrates that when Rasulullah(s) ascended to the heavens, he saw the following lines inscribed on the side of the Throne:

"There is no god but God, Muhammad is My servant and messenger, whom I have strengthened with Ali (as)."

Hence, Allah revealed this verse as a reference to what Rasulullah(s) had witnessed in the heavens. In the above verse, Imam Ali(as) is not only referred to as Allah's help but a firm believer as well.

Sources: *The Luminous Flashes* (227th & 228th Name), *Al-Burhan*, vol.2, p.91

Reflections

Use this space to pen down your precious thoughts.

Epilogue

"And they ask you (Muhammad) concerning **the orphans**. Say, 'It is better to set right their affairs, and if you associate with them, they are of course your brothers.'"

—SURAH AL BAQARA, VERSE: 220

Our aim with this book was to explore Imam Ali's (as) title, "The Father of Orphans," through a Qur'anic lens. It is important to understand that orphans of every community worldwide have a unique set of challenges and needs. They aren't limited to food and shelter; they extend to one's social well being, education, spiritual growth and health as well. We hope that with reflection on the traits ascribed to Imam Ali(as), our readers will be motivated to identify their own strengths and serve orphans around the world in whatever way they can.

Lastly, we would like to humbly request our readers to pray for the health and long life of the parents and children of our team members who diligently worked towards the completion of this book especially the **Ali, Hyder & Gallaghan** families. We would also request to recite Surah al-Fatiha for the following marhumins: **Sayyid Hashim Al Burhani, Syed Akhter Ali Moosavi, Munawar Ali Abbas and Mirza Khuda Quli Baig (Aijaz).**

www.ingramcontent.com/pod-product-compliance
Lightning Source LLC
Chambersburg PA
CBHW042036100526
44587CB00030B/4451